W9-COH-572

BIRDS

A TRUE BOOK

by

Melissa Stewart

Children's Press®
A Division of Grolier Publishing
New York London Hong Kong Sydney
Danbury, Connecticut

Horned puffins have brightly colored beaks.

Content Consultant
Kathy Carlstead, Ph.D.
National Zoological Park
Smithsonian Institution
Washington, D.C.

Jan Jenner, Ph.D.

The photograph on the cover shows a cedar waxwing eating a berry. The photograph on the title page shows a robin pulling a worm out of the ground.

Visit Children's Press® on the Internet at:
http://publishing.grolier.com

Library of Congress Cataloging-in-Publication Data

Stewart, Melissa.
  Birds / by Melissa Stewart.
    p. cm. — (A true book)
  Includes bibliographical references and index.
  Summary: Describes the basic behavior, physical traits, and life cycle of birds.
  ISBN: 0-516-22039-X (lib. bdg.)   0-516-25954-7 (pbk.)
  1. Birds—Juvenile literature. [1. Birds.] I. Title. II. Series.
QL676.2.S7525 2001
598—dc21   99-057542

GROLIER
PUBLISHING

©2001 Children's Press®,
A Division of Grolier Publishing Co., Inc.
All rights reserved. Published simultaneously in Canada.
Printed in the United States of America.
1 2 3 4 5 6 7 8 9 10 R 10 09 08 07 06 05 04 03 02 01

Contents

What Is a Bird?   5

Feathers Make Birds Special   8

How Birds Fly   16

Facts about Food   22

A Bird's Life   30

Birds in Our Lives   40

To Find Out More   44

Important Words   46

Index   47

Meet the Author   48

An eagle searches for food (top). A crow caws for its mate (above). A group of penguins slide down a snowbank (left).

What Is a Bird?

What do a soaring eagle, a
cawing crow, and a playful
penguin have in common?
They each have a backbone,
two legs, and two wings.
Their bodies are covered
with feathers, and they have
a beak instead of a mouth.
These are the features that

make birds different from all other groups of living things.

There are more than 9,000 different kinds of birds on Earth. Some are very large, and some are very small. Many ostriches are taller than a basketball player and weigh as much as 350 pounds (159 kilograms). They are too large to fly, but they can out-run most enemies. The bee hummingbird is the smallest bird in the world.

This bee hummingbird is about to take a sip of flower nectar.

It is smaller than most butter-flies and weighs less than a nickel. These tiny birds can fly backward and hover over flowers.

Feathers Make Birds Special

A bird's most special feature is its feathers. Feathers are made of the same material as your hair and fingernails. They grow out of little tubes in a bird's skin. Feathers help a bird fly, stay warm and dry, hide from enemies, and attract mates.

During the winter, a blue jay fluffs its feathers to stay warm and dry.

There are two major kinds of feathers—down feathers and contour feathers. Down feathers are like thermal underwear. Short, fluffy down

Look closely at these yellow warbler chicks (left). Do you see their down feathers? This contour feather (below) is from a blue jay.

feathers trap warm air close to a bird's skin. Contour feathers lie on top of the down feathers. They cover a bird's body, wings, and tail. They give a bird its shape and color.

A bird spends a lot of time preening, or taking care of, its feathers. It uses its feet and beak to comb the feathers so they lie flat. Preening also removes dirt and insects from

This great egret is preening.

the feathers. In addition, many birds take dust baths to remove mites, lice, and fleas from their bodies.

As a bird preens, it also rubs oil over its feathers. The oil is made in glands near the bird's tail. It makes the feathers waterproof. When the bird gets wet, the water rolls off the oily surface. This helps a bird stay dry and warm.

When a bird loses a feather, a new one grows in. Most birds

The anhinga uses its long, pointed bill to rub oil on its feathers. You can see its oil gland just above its tail.

oil gland

lose their feathers a few at a time, but ducks and geese molt. They lose all the feathers they need to fly once a year. When they molt, ducks and geese must stay hidden to avoid their enemies.

Sometimes a bird's new feathers are colored differently than the old ones. This is why young herring gulls and roseate spoonbills look different from the adult birds.

Bright and Beautiful

A male cardinal's bright red feathers (right) are easier to see than the female's light brown feathers (left).

Have you ever wondered why a male cardinal is bright red, but a female is mostly light brown? Many male birds have showy colors, while most females do not. A male uses his bright colors to attract a mate and to lure predators away from the nest. The female's drab colors blend in with her surroundings so predators cannot spot her while she is sitting on a nest.

How Birds Fly

If a bird did not have feathers, it could not fly. Each feather in a bird's body is controlled by a specific set of muscles. A bird uses its tail feathers to steer, slow down, and keep its balance. Meanwhile, air flows smoothly over the wing feathers.

This white tern uses its feathers to fly.

To take off, a bird jumps in the air, spreads its wings, and flaps them up and down. The curved shape of the wings

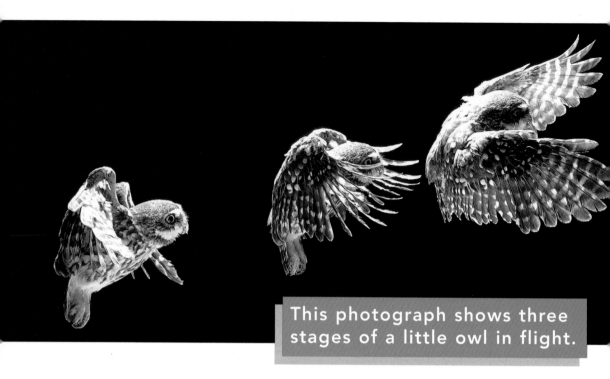

This photograph shows three stages of a little owl in flight.

lifts the bird upward. Most birds flap their wings as they fly, but eagles and hawks can glide, or soar. To land, a bird stops flapping its wings, spreads them out, and uses its wings and tail like a parachute.

The shape of a bird's wings determines how fast it can fly. The fastest birds can fly more than 100 miles (160 kilometers) per hour. No other kind of animal can travel as fast as birds.

A flock of sulphur-crested cockatoos in flight

How Birds Fly

To understand how birds fly, try this activity. Cut a piece of paper about 2 inches (5 centimeters) wide and 6 inches (15 cm) long. Hold one corner of the strip of paper between the thumb and forefinger of each hand. Blow over the top of the paper. The free end will lift up. By blowing, you make the air on the upper surface of the paper move quickly. As the fast-flowing air moves, it sucks the paper up. The slower-moving air on the lower surface pushes up, helping lift the paper.

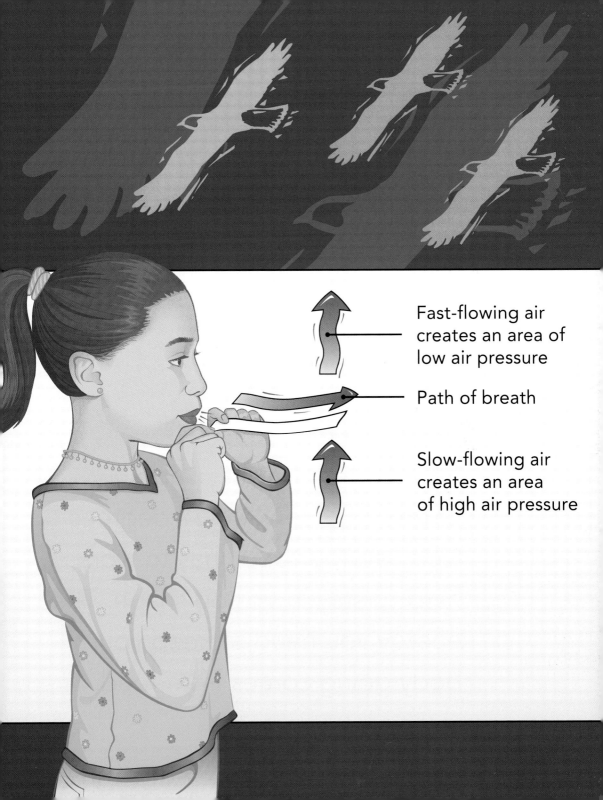

Fast-flowing air creates an area of low air pressure

Path of breath

Slow-flowing air creates an area of high air pressure

Facts About Food

Your heart beats 70 to 90 times in a minute, you breathe about 12 times in a minute, and your body temperature is usually about 98.6 degrees Fahrenheit (37 degrees Celsius). Your body has to work hard to stay in tip-top shape. The energy you need to keep your body going comes from food.

A song sparrow taking a bath

A hummingbird's heart may beat up to 1,260 times in a minute. A sparrow may breathe as many as 250 times in a minute. Most birds have a body temperature between 104 and 108°F (40 and 42°C). A bird's body needs a lot of energy to keep it going, so a bird must eat a lot of food to get the energy it needs. In fact, a kinglet may eat one-third of its body weight in a day.

Birds spend almost all their time looking for and eating food. Birds eat many types of foods. Woodpeckers and swallows eat insects. Toucans

This red-bellied woodpecker is eating a grasshopper.

The great blue heron uses its long, sharp bill to catch fish.

and parrots prefer fruit. Other birds eat fish, nuts and seeds, or plants. Some kinds of birds will eat almost anything.

You can tell what a bird eats by looking at the shape of its beak. A great blue heron uses its long, sharp bill to stab fish. A cardinal uses its short, strong beak to crack open sunflower seeds. An owl uses its hooked beak like a knife.

A bird's feet can also help you figure out what it eats and

An African jacana's long toes make it possible for this bird to walk across water plants.

how it hunts. An eagle uses its sharp, curved claws to catch and hold snakes, small mammals, and other birds. When an African jacana spreads out its 3-inch (8-cm) long toes, it can walk across water lilies in search of food. A chickadee holds sunflower seeds between its toes and bangs them against a hard surface until the shell breaks open.

A Bird's Life

Every bird begins life inside an egg with a hard shell. Most mother birds lay a clutch of one to ten eggs in a nest. The mother or father sits on the eggs to keep them warm as the young birds develop. Most eggs hatch 2 to 3 weeks after they are laid.

A female red grouse guards eggs at its nest. The eggs are colored to match their surroundings.

Most of the ostrich eggs in this nest are larger than softballs.

Eggs come in all sizes, shapes, and colors. A hummingbird's egg is as small as a pearl. An ostrich's egg may be up to 8 inches (20 cm) long. Because many animals eat bird eggs, most eggs are colored to match their surroundings. This makes it hard for predators to spot them.

Many kinds of chicks are helpless when they hatch. Their eyes are closed and they have no feathers. Their

A yellow warbler feeds its hungry chicks.

parents must feed them until they are old enough to find their own food. Most young birds can fly by the time they are 5 weeks old. By summer, most of the birds born in the spring can survive on their own. They spend their days searching for food.

This young robin is learning to survive on its own.

Many Canada geese migrate south for the winter.

In late summer or early fall, many North American birds migrate, or travel, to warmer parts of the world. They travel south to find more food. In spring, the birds fly north and start new families.

Most small birds live less than 5 years, but owls and hawks may live 60 years. Cockatoos may live more than 100 years.

How Do Birds Know

Scientists are not sure how birds find their way to their northern and southern homes. Birds that travel during the day may follow rivers, mountains, or other landmarks. Birds that fly at night may use stars or the moon as a guide.

Some birds make very long flights. The Swainson's hawk travels more than 7,000 miles (11,265 km) from the western United States to Argentina. The Pacific golden plover may travel more than 35 hours straight as it migrates from Alaska to Hawaii.

Where to Go?

A Swainson's hawk rests at the top of a tree in Yellowstone National Park.

Birds in Our Lives

Birds play an important role in our lives. People all over the world eat birds. In North America, many people eat chickens and turkeys. Their meat is high in protein and low in fat. Some people keep canaries, parrots, and other kinds of birds as pets.

Some people keep birds, such as this parakeet (right), as pets. Chicken (below) can be a tasty meal.

Other people enjoy watching birds in their backyards or in the woods.

Many people enjoy watching birds in their natural habitat.

Birds are also an important part of many ecosystems on Earth. Some animals eat birds. They are an important source of food for many reptiles and mammals. Birds destroy harmful insects and spread plant seeds to new places. When we pollute the water and air or kill too many birds, it can affect many other kinds of creatures. Let's hope that many different kinds of birds can continue to survive and fill our world with their songs.

To Find Out More

Here are some additional resources to help you learn more about birds:

 **Books**

Griffin, Stephen A. and Elizabeth May Griffin. **Bird Watching for Kids.** NorthWord Press, 1995.

Harrison, George N. and Kit Harrison. **Backyard Birdwatching for Kids.** Willow Creek Press, 1997.

Markle, Sandra. **Outside and Inside Birds.** Atheneum Books for Young Readers, 1994.

Miller, Sara Swan. **Perching Birds of North America.** Franklin Watts, 1999.

_____. **Shorebirds: From Stilts to Sanderlings.** Franklin Watts, 2000.

_____. **Waterfowl: From Swans to Screamers.** Franklin Watts, 1999.

Spauling, Dean T. **Feeding Our Feathered Friends.** Lerner, 1997.

Williams, Nick. **How Birds Fly.** Benchmark Books, 1997.

Zeaman, John. **Birds: From Forest to Family Room.** Franklin Watts, 1999.

⟨💡⟩ Organizations and Online Sites

Building Songbird Boxes
http://www.ces.ncsu.edu/ nreos/forest/steward/ www16.html

Find instructions for building birdhouses for a number of common birds at this site.

Cornell Laboratory of Ornithology
http://www.ornith.cornell. edu

This is your chance to take part in an online bird-watching project. The site also features a bird of the week, a variety of bird projects, and information about how people can help protect the world's birds.

HawkWatch International
P.O. Box 660
Salt Lake City, UT
84110-0660
www.hawkwatch.org/

Dedicated to birds of prey, this organization offers students and classes the opportunity to adopt several species of raptors.

National Audubon Society
http://www.audubon.org

This site provides general information about bird-watching and bird conservation, including raptors, and provides links to other sites.

Peterson Online: Birds
http://www.petersononline. com/

Learn how to identify all kinds of North American birds at this site.

The Virtual Birder
http://www.virtualbirder. com

Everyone interested in birds will find something at this site, including pictures of rare birds, links to other birding sites, virtual tours, tips on how to find birds in your area, and much more.

Important Words

beak a hard, pointed structure on a bird's face; it acts as a bird's mouth and contains the bird's nostrils

clutch a nest of eggs or a brood of chicks

down feather one of the soft, fluffy feathers that helps keep a bird warm

contour feather one of the outer feathers that cover a bird's body, wings, and tail

gland an organ in the body that gives off a liquid

migrate to travel a long distance to find a mate or food

molt to lose old feathers and grow new ones

predator an animal that hunts other animals for food

preen to clean and rub oil on feathers

Index

(**Boldface** page numbers
   indicate illustrations.)

African jacana, **28,** 29
anhinga, **13**
backbone, 5
beak, 5, 11
bee hummingbird, 6, 7
bird watching, 42, **42**
birds as food, 40, **41**
birds as pets, 40, **41**
body temperature (birds),
   24
cardinals, 15, **15,** 27
chicks, 33, **34**
contour feathers, 9, **10**
down feathers, 9–10, **10**
dust baths, 12
eagles, 18, 29
eggs, 30, **31, 32,** 33
enemies, 8, 13
feathers, 5, 8, 9, **9,**
   11–14, **14,** 16, **17,** 33
feet, 11, 27

food, 22, 24–29, 35, 37,
   43
great blue heron, **26,** 27
great egret, **11**
hawks, 18, 37
herring gulls, 14
how birds fly, 20–21
legs, 5
mates, 8, 15
migrate, **36,** 37, 38
molt, 13
nest, 15, 30, **31, 32**
oil, 12, **13**
ostriches, 6, **32,** 33
owls, **18,** 27, 37
predators, 15, 33
preening, 11, **11,** 12
roseate spoonbills, 14, **14**
sparrow, 23, **23**
tail, 10, 12, **13,** 16, 18
wings, 5, 10, 16, 17, 18,
   19
woodpecker, 24, **24**

Meet the Author

Melissa Stewart earned a Bachelor's Degree in biology from Union College and a Master's Degree in Science and Environmental Journalism from New York University. She has been writing about science and nature for almost a decade. Ms. Stewart lives in Danbury, Connecticut.